SIMON WOOTTON
& TERRY HORNE

strategic
thinking

●●● a step-by-step approach
to strategy

SECOND EDITION

The Association of MBAS

KOGAN
PAGE

London and Sterling, VA

First published as *Strategic Planning: the Nine Step Programme* in 1997

Second edition 2001
Reprinted 2001 (twice), 2003, 2004

Kogan Page Ltd
120 Pentonville Road
London N1 9JN
UK
www.kogan–page.co.uk

Kogan Page US
22883 Quicksilver Drive
Sterling VA 20166–2012
USA

British Library Cataloguing in Publication Data
A CIP record for this book is available from the British Library
ISBN 0 7494 32187

Typeset by Saxon Graphics Ltd, Derby
Printed and bound in the USA by Thomson–Shore, Inc

Contents

Preface

This book is not for creative entrepreneurs, born leaders or those blessed with the gift of prophecy. It is for ordinary mortals who are asked to manage strategy or write strategic plans. It is for those who prefer to think things out, one step at a time. The thinking skills required were identified during a seven-year study, which began in 1989, working with Roger Armstrong, at the University of Central Lancashire. The way in which thinking skills can be developed, deployed and sequenced, in order to deliver Applied Thinking, has been modelled by the Noetic Institute. The results of applying these models to decision making, problem solving, developing intelligence and learning from experience, will be jointly published in 2004 as *Applied Thinking* by The Noetic Institute (www.noeticinstitute.com) and Libra Press. This book examines the results of applying the models to the problem of formulating strategy and writing plans. Applied Thinking involves the deployment of five basic, four combinations and three higher order applied thinking skills. The five basic thinking skills are Recollective Thinking and Memory; Visual Thinking and Imagination; Numerical Thinking and Mathematics; Emotional Thinking and Empathy, plus Conversational Thinking and Language. The Four Combination Thinking Skills are Ethical Thinking and Morality; Symbolic Thinking and Schema; Predictive Thinking and Forecasting, plus Metaphorical Thinking and Systems. The Three Higher Order applied thinking skills are Critical, Creative and Reflective Thinking. The activities involved in developing a strategy have been divided into three areas: making sense of information; formatting ideas, and planning action. Each area involves three steps and the use of different thinking skills. Some examples of the use of different thinking skills are:

▌ recollective and predictive – eg analysing the impact of technology, economies, markets, politics, law, ethics and social trends;

▌ numerical and critical when auditing capability;

▌ recollective and reflective – eg inferring threats and opportunities;

▌ visual and predictive – eg making forecasts;

▌ emotional and metaphorical – eg writing a mission statement;

▌ creative and conversational – eg devising ways to fulfil missions;

▌ ethical and critical – eg evaluating the economics, efficiency, effectiveness, ethics, feasibility and risk of available options;

▌ emotional and metaphorical – eg assessing social and environmental implications;

▌ visual and symbolically – eg presenting the implementation plan.

Readers will learn about the theories behind strategy, strategic planning and strategic management, through activity and practice. They get practice in using the

12 component thinking skills. These are highly portable skills. Readers learn to adapt their thinking as circumstances change. These are skills they will need not only as strategists and entrepreneurs, but as citizens and lifelong learners in a changing world. Because the learning is self-managed, it promotes self-confidence and self-reliance.

The book has been highly rated by managers of large multi-national companies and by managers of small to medium-sized enterprises in the UK engineering industry, and in UK public-service organisations. It has proved popular with final year undergraduates and first-year MBA students of business and management. It is fully internationalised and rooted in contemporary thinking on prescriptive, emergent and critical approaches to strategy. It has been adopted as the core text in strategic management in Business Schools in Asia, Eastern Europe and South America.

Strategic thinking – an introduction

Strategic thinking involves three activities: making sense of information, formulating ideas and planning action. Each activity involves three steps, each step involves different combinations of thinking skills. When you can confidently use all the thinking skills involved then you can think strategically.

Making sense involves thinking predicatively about changes in technology, economics, markets, politics, law, ethics and society, and then numerically and critically when auditing the strategic capability of an organisation. A framework for this is provided. Newly gathered information needs to 'make sense' in the light of what you already know. This involves recollection and reflection.

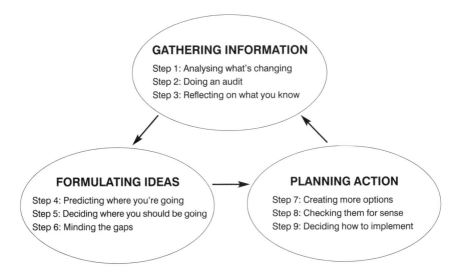

GATHERING INFORMATION
Step 1: Analysing what's changing
Step 2: Doing an audit
Step 3: Reflecting on what you know

FORMULATING IDEAS
Step 4: Predicting where you're going
Step 5: Deciding where you should be going
Step 6: Minding the gaps

PLANNING ACTION
Step 7: Creating more options
Step 8: Checking them for sense
Step 9: Deciding how to implement

Formulating ideas involves thinking about the future. Because it is hard, if not impossible, to obtain clear and certain information about the future, we have to use thinking skills which we use when gathering and assessing information about the past or the present. These thinking skills involve forecasting, prediction, imagination and visual thinking, as well as critical evaluation.

Planning action involves thinking creatively about the possible actions to take. Options can be evaluated numerically, ethically and empathetically, when thinking about their desirability. The thinking skills required for strategic thinking combine with the conversational skills required to implement strategic change, to produce a model of the strategic management process. This model is taken from *A Thoughtful Approach to the Practice of Management*, Horne and Doherty, 2002, Routledge.

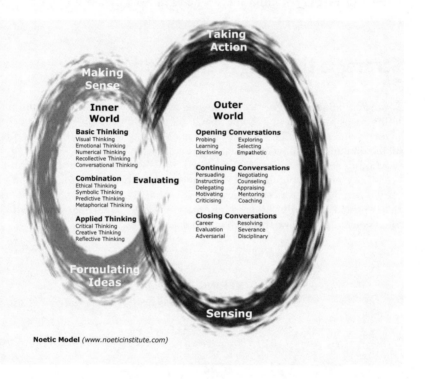

Noetic Model *(www.noeticinstitute.com)*

Step 1

Analyse what's changing

Will help you to:

- Identify new openings and opportunities

- Identify dangers or problems

- Decide whether there is a need for change

KNOWING WHAT IS CHANGING OUT THERE

'Temples' is a mnemonic[1] for things that are changing in the areas of:

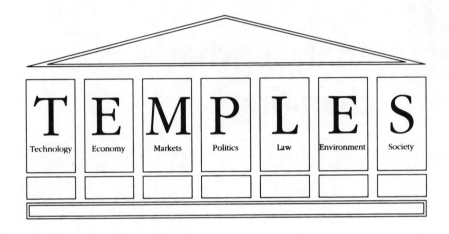

---

1. The authors acknowledge the work of Gilly McHugh of Lancashire Business School who pioneered and tested this mnemonic.

External Problems and Opportunities

If you would find it helpful to do some prior thinking about what might be changing in the areas of technology, the economy, markets, politics, law, ethics and society, you could turn to the prompt sheets on pages 4 – 12 before completing this table.

What is changing in the areas of:	What are the likely problems and opportunities that will impact on your organisation in the:			
	Medium term		Long term	
	Problem	Opportunity	Problem	Opportunity
Technology				
Economy				
Markets				
Politics				
Law				
Ethics				
Society				

Prompt Sheet on Changes in Technology

▌ How will improvements in communication methods change the way you work with your customers, suppliers and employees?

▌ Will you be affected by CD ROMs or the World Wide Web?

▌ Will you be affected by telephone shopping and banking?

▌ What are the implications of new technology for training?

▌ How long before your current equipment becomes obsolete?

▌ What research and development is occurring in your industry?

▌ How will changes in transport affect you, eg:
  – Congested roads?
  – Motorway charges?
  – Increased air freight?
  – The channel tunnel?
  – Juggernaut lorries?

▌ Within the foreseeable future, could you, your employees, your customers and your suppliers increasingly work from home?

▌ What would be the implications for your business or the value of its property assets, especially if these are needed as security?

Prompt Sheet on Changes in the Economy

▪ How do movements in key economic indicators affect you, eg, rising unemployment, falling inflation, increasing imports?

▪ The exchange rate – does it impact on you or your customers?

▪ Is your organisation affected by the levels of consumer credit?

▪ Is your industry growing or declining in employment terms?

▪ Is your growth restricted by a shortage of skilled people?

▪ How are you affected by rising levels of consumer spending?

▪ Who has the spending power that affects you? Older people? Younger people? Public institutions?

▪ Which government departments have rising or falling budgets or spending plans and how will these affect you?

▪ How do your labour and employee costs and productivity compare with Pacific Rim countries and China?

▪ Do you understand the concept of Fair Trade? Does it have implications for your own marketing or purchasing policies?

Prompt Sheet on Changes in the Market

■ How large is the market? How many competitors are there?

■ Is your profitability linked to the scale of your operation, ie, in the main, do the larger businesses make more profit in this market than the smaller ones?

■ Would the effect of a small contraction be severe?

■ Is a great deal of capital required to enter this market? How easy would it be for a new entrant to find the initial capital?

■ Does your business need particular channels of distribution? If so, are they vulnerable to becoming controlled by a competitor or by another organisation that could 'hold you to ransom'?

■ Does your organisation provide services or goods that are unique? How could your customers obtain the benefits they get from your unique service in quite another way?

■ How easily could someone copy what you do?

■ Do you have patents, copyright or licence agreements that will expire within the period of this plan?

■ Are you dependent on only a few suppliers?

■ Is it possible they might merge?

■ How easy would it be for you to switch to other suppliers?

■ Where are the nearest alternative sources of supply?

■ How easily could your major customers find better prices, performance, designs, ease of access or just a more widely advertised and promoted service?

▌ About how many organisations are supplying your product or service (locally and nationally) and what is their size range?

▌ Is most of the business done by only a few organisations?

▌ To what degree are your services or products 'substitutable'?

▌ Is the total business being done by you and your competitors growing or contracting?

▌ How do your competitors set about getting business?

▌ Is the main strength of your competitors the dependability of their service, or how easy they make life for customers?

▌ Do your competitors provide a range of goods or services that totally meet your customers' needs and wants?

▌ Are your competitors quick to sense your customers' changing needs and to respond to them?

▌ Do your competitors seem to take a long or a short term view?

▌ What are your competitors' attitudes towards risk? Are they more prepared than you to be the first with something new?

▌ Do you think they are aiming to be the market leaders?

▌ What are your competitors best and worst at?

▌ Which word – developing, growing, maturing or declining – would best describe the kind of market in which your organisation is competing? Use the model overleaf to try to visualise the position of your organisation in your market:

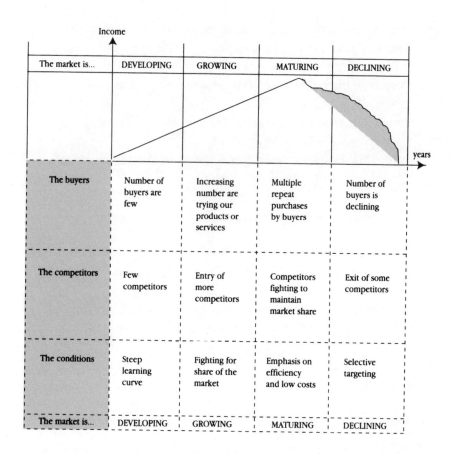

Income				
The market is...	DEVELOPING	GROWING	MATURING	DECLINING
The buyers	Number of buyers are few	Increasing number are trying our products or services	Multiple repeat purchases by buyers	Number of buyers is declining
The competitors	Few competitors	Entry of more competitors	Competitors fighting to maintain market share	Exit of some competitors
The conditions	Steep learning curve	Fighting for share of the market	Emphasis on efficiency and low costs	Selective targeting
The market is...	DEVELOPING	GROWING	MATURING	DECLINING

Prompt Sheet on Changes in Politics

▌ What new political decisions are likely, from the existing government or from a new government?

▌ What impact do the charters and standards being implemented by the government have on the development and maintenance of your business?

▌ Do you consider the government of the day a stable influence within whose policy decisions you can adequately plan?

▌ Is your organisation taking advantage of current taxation policies?

▌ Do you understand the government's foreign trade policies?

▌ Do you understand the government's foreign aid policies?

▌ How could political changes in overseas countries have implications for your customers or suppliers of raw materials, eg:

  – former eastern communist countries retreating from western market-based economies;

  – increased nationalism, leading to increases in the number and scale of armed conflicts;

  – increased use of trade sanctions and embargoes to exert international pressure over human rights or other issues;

  – the rise in religious militancy or the rejection of western cultural values by some Asian or Arab countries?

Prompt Sheet on Changes in the Law

▌ What new or proposed legislation might affect you?

▌ What legislation is affecting your organisation, eg:

  employment law;
  – environmental regulations;
  – health and safety legislation;
  – compulsory competitive tendering?

▌ What government departments are particularly relevant?

▌ Are they developing policies that could be of interest to you?

▌ What is your local authority trying to change, through its planning department, enterprise grants or training schemes?

▌ Are you affected by European Union (EU) regulations?

▌ How will the EU's 'Social Chapter' affect your organisation?

▌ Does existing legislation protect you from competition? Does it assist you against competitors? Do you see any changes that would make your position more or less secure?

Prompt Sheet on Changes in the Environment

▐ Will 'green' issues affect your organisation?

▐ Are your major competitors selling a 'green' image?

▐ Are you recycling where possible?

▐ Do you look after your staff's health and welfare?

▐ Are you considering altering your sources of raw materials?

▐ Is your research and development department researching new ways of doing things?

▐ What pressure groups are, or might become, interested in the activities of your organisation?

▐ Have you checked out the implications of 'sick building' syndrome for your organisation?

▐ Do you monitor stress levels in your employees and do you have a stress management policy?

▐ Are your employees involved in discussions about flexible patterns of work and holidays?

▐ Do you understand how your policies on sourcing and using energy and fuels impact on the environment?

▐ Will increasing concern over carbon dioxide emissions, solvent use, the quality of air, water and food, and fears about climatic change have any impact on you or your customers or your suppliers?

▐ Will you be affected by pressure groups advocating Fair Trading and Human Rights issues?

▐ How will agreement on Fair Trading and Human Rights issues affect you, your customers and your suppliers?

Prompt Sheet on Changes in Society

▮ Do your employees and customers expect to be involved in decisions that affect them?

▮ What impact does this have on your organisation's communications, negotiations and possible management structures?

▮ How many people expect an improving quality of life at work, at home and in the general environment?

▮ Is concern over burglary, vandalism, homelessness and car crimes likely to affect your employees, your customers or your business?

▮ How will changing family patterns (eg, higher proportions of one-parent families, divorces, families where husband and wife are both employed, over-65s with no families to support them) influence your decisions?

▮ Will part-time working, short-term contracts and sub-contracting become increasingly important to your business?

▮ Will changes in leisure, holidays and lifestyle affect you?

STEP 1 SUMMARY

Step 1 will have helped you to:

▮ Identify new openings and opportunities

▮ Identify dangers or problems

▮ Identify whether there is a need for change

Step 2

Doing an audit

Will help you to:

▌ Highlight features of products or services

▌ Highlight advantages over competitors

▌ Identify benefits to customers

DOING AN AUDIT – THE AREAS TO CONSIDER

The 12 Ms relate to things that are relevant to your organisation. They are:

M arket reputation

M ental agility

M anagement

M onitoring

M otivation

M ovement

M anpower

M achines

M aterials

M orale

M oney

M ores

If you would find it helpful to do some prior thinking about these areas, you could turn to the prompt sheets on pages 16–44 before completing the table opposite.

Internal Problems and Opportunities

What is changing in the areas of:	What are the likely problems and opportunities that will impact on your organisation in the:			
	Medium term		Long term	
	Problem	Opportunity	Problem	Opportunity
Market reputation				
Money				
Manpower				
Machines				
Materials				
Mental agility				
Management				
Morale				
Mores				
Monitoring				
Motivation				
Movement				

Prompt Sheet on **M** arket Reputation

The main features of your product	In what way are these superior or inferior to competitors?	Which are important to your customers?	Why?

Features could include such things as:

space it takes up

availability

workmanship

reliability

quality

quantity

accessibility

cost

desirability

power

delivery times

reputation

credibility

From the previous table on page 16:

In which features that are important to your customers do you think you have an advantage over your competitors?	How do they benefit customers? How do they help customers to feel better?

Identifying who your customers are will allow you to provide services or products that they want and this will help you remain in business, increase profits and keep ahead of the competition. Use the following questions to help you evaluate who your customers are:

▌ Where do you operate, provide services or sell products?

▌ What are the characteristics of the people who are likely to buy your goods or use your services?

▌ How many customers do you have?

▌ How many potential customers are there?

▌ Why do they do business with you?

▌ What features of your products or services do they like most?

▌ How do your customers think your service could be improved?

▌ Does your organisation cope well with customer complaints?

▌ Could your products or services be sold in other sectors of the market or elsewhere in the world?

The best way to get a 'feel' for your customers is to go and talk to them and ask them about their needs and concerns.

Prompt Sheet on **M**oney

a) Know your organisation's financial performance

Get your accountant to complete the table below for your organisation, or do it yourself, using your own copy of the organisation's accounts for the last three years. You may find the prompt sheets on pages 30–44 helpful.

Ratio	Calculation	Ratio for year		
Return on net assests (%)	$\dfrac{\text{Profit (before interest and tax)}}{\text{Total capital employed in business}} \times 100$			
Profit margin (%)	$\dfrac{\text{Profit (before interest and tax)}}{\text{Sales or income}} \times 100$			
Net asset turnover	$\dfrac{\text{Sales or income}}{\text{Total net assets employed in business}}$			
Debt ratio (%)	$\dfrac{\text{Long-term loans}}{\text{Total capital employed}} \times 100$			
Interest cover	$\dfrac{\text{Profit (before interest and tax)}}{\text{Interest on long-term loans}}$			
Current ratio	$\dfrac{\text{Current assets}}{\text{Current liabilities}}$			
Liquidity ratio	$\dfrac{\text{Liquid assets}}{\text{Current liabilities}}$			

b)   Know about your organisation's cash flow

Complete a cash flow forecast using the table on the following two pages:

1. Under 'cash balance', enter the overall overdraft or cash held at the end of the previous period.

2. Make a note of any receipts or income that you expect to receive.

3. Make a note of payments that you expect to make; a checklist of likely items is shown in the table.

4. The receipts less payments for the month will give you the net cash flow (F) for the month, ie (F = R – P). If you add the cash balance (C = B + F), this will indicate how much cash is left in the organisation at the end of that month. The figure 'C' becomes the opening balance for month 2, and the process is repeated.

5. Complete a cash flow forecast for the next two years using the table on page 22.

Cash Flow Forecast

Month	1	2	3	4	5	6
Cash balance (B)						
Expected receipts in:						
Owners' investment						
Loans (from…)						
Cash payments						
Earlier sales						
Selling of assets						
Interest received						
Grants						
Other income						
Total receipts in (R)						
Expected payments out:						
Premium on lease						
Purchase of property						
Purchase of fittings						
Raw materials						
Payment for goods						
Employees' net wages						
Income tax and NI						
Training expenses						
Rent and rates						
Fuel (gas and electricity)						
Telephone						
Postage						
Printing and stationery						
Subscriptions & periodicals						
Advertising						
Repairs and maintenance						
Vehicle and travel costs						
Insurances						
Professional fees						
Loan repayments						
Bank charges						
Bank interest						
Value Added Tax						
Corporation Tax						
Other cash going out						
Total payments out (P)						
Receipts in less payments out = cash flow (F) = R-P						
Cash remaining in the business (C) =B+F						

Month	7	8	9	10	11	12	Total
Cash balance (B)							
Expected receipts in:							
Owners' investment							
Loans (from…)							
Cash payments							
Earlier sales							
Selling of assets							
Interest received							
Grants							
Other income							
Total receipts in (R)							
Expected payments out:							
Premium on lease							
Purchase of property							
Purchase of fittings							
Raw materials							
Payment for goods							
Employees' net wages							
Income tax and NI							
Training expenses							
Rent and rates							
Fuel (gas and electricity)							
Telephone							
Postage							
Printing and stationery							
Subscriptions & periodicals							
Advertising							
Repairs and maintenance							
Vehicle and travel costs							
Insurances							
Professional fees							
Loan repayments							
Bank charges							
Bank interest							
Value Added Tax							
Corporation Tax							
Other cash going out							
Total payments out (P)							
Receipts in less payments out = cash flow (F) = R-P							
Cash remaining in the business (C) =B+F							

Year and quarter	2/1	2/2	2/3	2/4	3/1	3/2	3/4
Cash balance (B)							
Expected receipts in:							
Owners' investment							
Loans (from…)							
Cash payments							
Earlier sales							
Selling of assets							
Interest received							
Grants							
Other income							
Total receipts in (R)							
Expected payments out:							
Premium on lease							
Purchase of property							
Purchase of fittings							
Raw materials							
Payment for goods							
Employees' net wages							
Income tax and NI							
Training expenses							
Rent and rates							
Fuel (gas and electricity)							
Telephone							
Postage							
Printing and stationery							
Subscriptions & periodicals							
Advertising							
Repairs and maintenance							
Vehicle and travel costs							
Insurances							
Professional fees							
Loan repayments							
Bank charges							
Bank interest							
Value Added Tax							
Corporation Tax							
Other cash going out							
Total payments out (P)							
Receipts in less payments out = cash flow (F) = R-P							
Cash remaining in the business (C) =B+F							

To review your cash flow forecast, look at the bottom line in each period. Are any of these figures negative? If so, when that period is reached, the organisation will be unable to pay its bills. You will need to increase your sources of funding, or reduce your outgoings, or both. If the bottom line is always positive, you should plan to invest the surplus in some way. Your cash flow has implications for your choice of strategy. For example, if a particular strategy involves extra staff training, you will have to check whether you have sufficient cash.

c) Understand your profit and loss account and balance sheet

The following table will help you understand how a profit and loss account is constructed.

Constructing a profit and loss account

Sales/income

less:	The cost of producing the goods or services sold	=	*the gross profit*
less:	Depreciation, selling costs, administration costs	=	*profit before interest and tax*
less:	Any interest on loans (if applicable)	=	*the profit before tax*
less:	Any tax due	=	*the profit after tax*
less:	Any dividends declared	=	*the retained profits (sometimes called retained earnings)*

Constructing a balance sheet

	Fixed assets	(original cost of land, property, buildings, plant and equipment, less depreciation)
plus:	Current assets	(current value of stock, debtors, cash and investments)
less:	Current liabilities	(overdrafts plus any money you owe that must be paid within one year)
equals	Net assets	
	Long-term loans	(money you owe that need not be repaid in less than one year)
plus:	Shareholders' funds	(money put in by you or shareholders plus accumulated retained profits)
equals	Total capital employed	(this should equal the value of net assets)

For the purpose of strategic planning in your organisation, you should concentrate on two aspects:

1. Performance – is your organisation trading successfully? Is your organisation making good use of your money? Would you be better off selling up and putting the money in a building society? Would you get a better return? Less hassle? Less risk?

2. Financial health – is your organisation financially healthy? Is there going to be enough cash to pay the bills?

These can be understood by looking at performance ratios and financial health ratios.

Performance ratios

Calculation

1. For each £100 of your money, how much are you getting?

$$\frac{\text{Profit (before interest and before tax)}}{\text{Total capital employed in the business}} \times 100$$

(called return on net assets – RONA, or return on capital employed – ROCE)

2. For each £100 of income coming in, how much is profit?

$$\frac{\text{Profit (before interest and tax)}}{\text{Sales or income}} \times 100$$

(often called profit margin, %)

3. How many times in one year does the money get used?

$$\frac{\text{Sales or income}}{\text{Total money employed in the business}} \times 100$$

The return on net assets (or the return on capital employed) is a measure of how well the organisation is performing as a trading concern. It is an effective yardstick by which your organisation's financial performance can be assessed. This ratio is particularly useful when it is examined in the light of the two ratios that comprise it: the *profit margin*, which is the proportion of sales or income represented by the profits (before interest and tax) and the *turnover of the capital employed* (or the turnover of net assets), which tells you whether or not you are making enough use of the money tied up in the business.

If you decide that you want to improve your return on the money that you have tied up in the business, there are two possible implications for your strategic planning. Either profitability must be increased, or capital employed must be reduced. By looking at how these two ratios have been changing during the last few years, you can adopt a strategic approach that better meets your organisation's needs for the future.

Financial health

The financial health tests are of two kinds: tests for solvency – will the loans be called in? and tests for liquidity – will you be able to pay your bills/salaries on time?

Tests for solvency		
The debt ratio	equals	$\dfrac{\text{Long-term loans}}{\text{Total capital employed}}$
The interest cover ratio	equals	$\dfrac{\text{Profit (before interest and tax)}}{\text{Interest on long-term loans}}$

The *debt ratio* is sometimes called 'gearing'. It shows how much of your business is being funded by the owners (sometimes called 'equity capital' or 'shareholders' funds') and how much of the business is being funded by borrowed money. Loans generally have fixed interest payments that must be paid regardless of your profit levels, whereas owners or shareholders expect to get a higher return (or 'dividend') when profits go up and may have to accept a lower dividend at times when profits are not so good.

The *interest cover* shows by how many times the interest payments are covered by profits, so it is a measure of your safety margin. If profits are ten times your interest payments, then you can survive your profits dropping to one tenth of their present level without getting into trouble with the bank.

Tests for liquidity		
The current ratio	equals	$\dfrac{\text{Current assets}}{\text{Current liabilities}}$
The liquidity ratio	equals	$\dfrac{\text{Liquid assets}}{\text{Current liabilities}}$

The *current ratio* shows the relationship between current assets and current liabilities. If the ratio is high, this means that there is a high level of current assets to liabilities and that there should be little difficulty in meeting the organisation's debts as they become due. It is important to look at how the figure has changed when compared with the previous year, rather than the figure itself. A decrease in relation to the previous year's figures would be a warning sign. It is also worth noting that while a high current ratio denotes strong financial stability, it may also indicate poor asset usage!

The *liquidity ratio* shows the proportion of funds that can easily be turned into cash to pay the bills. A shortage of cash may push the organisation towards increased borrowings, and this in turn increases the interest payments. Beyond a certain point, the requests for increased borrowings will be refused and bankruptcy looms.

Prompt Sheet on **M**anpower

▌ Do you have a multi-skilled labour force?

▌ Is your labour force flexible in what it can do and is willing to do?

▌ Do you have adequately trained staff?

▌ Will your staff work across several functions?

▌ Have you a readily available source of labour?

▌ Do you provide career training?

▌ Do you encourage your staff to further their education?

▌ Do you undertake performance appraisal?

▌ Do you set objectives for staff members and for teams?

▌ Do you require any specialised staff who are hard to come by?

▌ How do you seek to recruit and retain these people?

▌ Are there any training grants and employment grants that you could take advantage of and are you doing so?

▌ How does the EU employment law affect your organisation?

▌ Is your staff turnover high or low?

▌ In either case, might it cause you a problem?

▌ Do all your staff have personal development plans?

Prompt Sheet on **M**achines

▪ How soon will your machines need replacing?

▪ Do you have a comprehensive maintenance schedule?

▪ Are there newer and better machines available to do the job?

▪ Can you obtain replacement parts easily and quickly?

▪ Are there times when your machines stand idle?

▪ Have you considered putting them to use for other purposes?

▪ Are there grants available to help you purchase, lease or develop equipment?

▪ What effect will health and safety laws have on your machinery?

▪ Are your operations heavily automated?

▪ Do any machines cause quality control problems?

▪ Is your communications equipment user-friendly?

▪ Are all calls diverted so that callers always get an answer?

▪ Does it record messages 24 hours a day, and record callers' numbers, to make it easier for you to call back?

▪ Does it give help-line numbers for out-of-hours backup?

▪ Does it tell you when you have a customer waiting on an outside line?

▪ Will it divert to mobile phones or bleeps for staff on call?

▪ Does it have built-in fax and e-mail?

▪ Does it have conferencing for multi-person conversations?

▪ Does it monitor the frequency customers get 'engaged' or how long they wait?

Prompt Sheet on **M**aterials

▌ Do you do trial runs of new products or services?

▌ Are you reliant on someone else doing it for you?

▌ Do you do your own packaging? Does it look professional? Does it protect the product or promote the service?

▌ Are there several suppliers of your raw materials?

▌ Are there alternative sources of raw materials?

▌ Are you tied to one supplier?

▌ Are the prices of your materials affected by the exchange rate?

▌ Could you work with other organisations to achieve a discount through group purchasing or bulk buying?

▌ Do you receive generous credit terms from suppliers?

▌ Do you have patents and copyrights on your products?

▌ Do you control your stock levels effectively and efficiently?

▌ Are your suppliers supplying you at just a sufficient level for smooth running, or are you always over-stocked?

▌ Do you return faulty deliveries quickly?

▌ Does your organisation order goods effectively and efficiently?

▌ Do you have a long lead-up time to producing new services?

▮ Do you operate a policy of Fair Trading?

▮ Are you aware of the implications of Fair Trading for your purchasing and supplies?

▮ Could you benefit by working more closely with suppliers – especially those who supply your most innovative competitors?

Prompt Sheet on **M**ental Agility

■ Do your employees have sufficient problem-solving skills?

■ Are your employees flexible enough to cope with change?

■ Do your employees provide innovative ideas?

■ Do you encourage your employees to express their ideas?

■ Is your organisation proactive or reactive?

■ Does your organisation rely on one or two people for ideas and problem-solving, or is it a team effort?

■ Are the ideas practical or are they all 'pie in the sky'?

■ How does your research and development function interact with the rest of your organisation?

■ Does your organisation copy existing products, or are you the market leader with new ideas and products?

■ Do you encourage your employees to develop team skills?

■ Are your employees trained to be your organisation's antennae?

■ Are your employees trained to tune into your internal workings and to notice and report discord?

■ Are your employees encouraged to visualise future situations by using pictures, drawings, sketches and flipcharts?

■ Are your employees introduced to different ways of thinking about things and trained to know which to use?

▌ Are your employees encouraged to quantify what they are saying or thinking wherever possible?

▌ Are they aware of the impact of mood on mental efficiency and of the importance of a positive 'can do' disposition?

▌ Are your employees aware of the physical conditions needed for mental work, eg, ventilation, exercise and posture?

▌ Are your employees aware of the positive and negative effects on mental efficiency of nicotine? alcohol? caffeine?

▌ Have they been given information on the effects of diet and vitamin and mineral deficiencies on mental agility?

▌ Are you aware of the impact on mental agility of:

- smells;

- music;

- stress;

- diet;

- colours;

- sleep;

- air quality;

- photocopiers;

- lighting;

- computers;

- the clothes staff wear?

Prompt Sheet on **M**anagement

▮ Can your managers cope with the changing market?

▮ Do you have a sufficient number of managers?

▮ Do you have too many?

▮ If you took over another organisation, would you be able to use your existing managers?

▮ Does your organisation have sufficient financial management?

▮ Does your organisation have the necessary human resource or personnel management skills?

▮ Are your managers properly trained and equipped to undertake their current job and any future positions?

▮ Do you encourage mentoring and management development?

▮ Do your managers, between them, have a wide enough range of thinking skills and learning skills?

▮ Do your managers, between them, cover the range of skills and roles needed for effective team-working?

Prompt Sheet on **M**orale

▯ Do your employees feel safe in their jobs?

▯ Do your employees actively participate in your organisation?

▯ Are they the ones who come up with new ideas?

▯ Do you act on them?

▯ How do you reward your staff for these ideas?

▯ Do you reward only cost-saving ideas?

▯ How do you obtain grass roots feelings?

▯ What do you provide for the employees other than a salary?

▯ Have you given everyone the level of choice and decision-making power that they want over their work content and when and where they do it, consistent with retaining appropriate monitoring and control and concern for safety?

▯ Are employees involved in the choice of equipment they use, or the decor of their work environment?

▯ Do senior managers regularly walk through, or visit, the places where their employees are working?

▯ Are all notice boards clean, up-to-date and free from graffiti?

▯ Are walkways and fire escape routes kept clear at all times?

▯ Do employees automatically remove any litter they find?

❙ Do employees support the organisation's social events?

❙ Do employees form and enter teams in competitions?

❙ Do employees meet outside the work environment?

❙ Do employees work flexibly to cover for each other and are they mutually supportive and helpful?

❙ Are dress codes and standards of personal appearance high?

❙ Are employees proactive in approaching customers and seeking new work and business?

Prompt Sheet on **M**ores

▮ What sort of management values does your organisation have: 'don't rock the boat', 'roll with the punches', 'plan ahead', 'dream ahead'?

▮ What is your organisation's focus: internal or external?

▮ What triggers your organisation to change: a crisis, unsatisfactory performance, anticipated problems, or continual search?

▮ How does your organisation cope with risk: reject it, accept it, seek it?

▮ What are your organisational goals: status quo, minimal disturbance, improve on past performance or seek the best?

▮ How does your organisation undertake problem-solving: through trial and error, diagnosis, anticipation or creativity?

▮ Where is the power focus in your organisation: in production, in marketing, in research and development, in multi-disciplinary teamwork, or in general management?

▮ How do you manage your systems: by policies and procedures, capital budgeting, long-range budgeting or strategic planning?

▮ What management information systems do you have: informal, formal, based on past performance or future potential?

▮ How do you survey what goes on outside your organisation: by doing nothing, forecasting or trend analysis?

▮ How is decision-making carried out: top-down, bottom-up, or devolved?

■   How does the culture affect what individuals do?

■   How does it affect your selection and promotion?

■   Do managers and employees have an outward-facing culture and reflect this in regular visits to customers and suppliers?

■   Does the management system create an atmosphere of working together or does it generate fragmentation?

Prompt Sheet on **M** onitoring

▪ Do you distinguish levels of control, eg, management control, operational control or strategic control in your organisation?

▪ Do you identify key result determinants and collect the relevant information to control them?

▪ Do you allow diversity of control – do you avoid using the same universal standards, such as sales volume, in all your departments?

▪ Do you monitor over a sensible time period?

▪ Are your measures misleading?

▪ Do you monitor 'negatively' to identify performance below plan or do you monitor both 'negatively' and 'positively'?

▪ Are your monitoring systems discussed with staff and altered after discussion, or are they 'top-down' implemented?

▪ Does your organisation cope well with customer complaints?

Prompt Sheet on ▉otivation

■ How do you reward your employees: by bonuses, management by objectives, performance appraisal, or by helping them devise a personal development plan?

■ How do you reward your suppliers?

■ How do you reward, delight and astonish your customers?

■ What is it about you that keeps customers coming back?

■ What drives your organisation: the CEO or the employees?

■ Do you know the major hobbies, activities, interests and strongly-held beliefs of all your employees?

■ Do you know, for each employee, the reasons why they work?

■ Accepting that the need to earn money may be the prime motivator for many, what thereafter is the relative importance of:

 – social contact;

 – belonging to a group;

 – feeling valued and needed;

 – obtaining recognition, admiration, achievement and applause?

■ Are your employees able to create:

 – their own ideas, products, or schemes;

 – their own office team?

- Are your employees able to control:

    - their working environment;

    - their working arrangements;

    - their choice of car?

Prompt Sheet on **M**ovement

▌ Do you own your own transport?

▌ If hired or leased, is it in your house style or livery?

▌ Would you be better buying in a 24-hour delivery service?

▌ Do you promote your delivery service in your literature?

▌ Do you always collect back faulty items from customers?

STEP 2 SUMMARY

Step 2 will have helped you to:

▌ Highlight features of products or services

▌ Highlight advantages over competitors

▌ Identify benefits to customers

Step 3

Reflecting on what you know

Will help you to:

■   Summarise an external appraisal

■   Summarise an internal audit

■   Make sense of the summary

GETTING IT TOGETHER

Reflect on the summary tables from the results of your 'Temples' external appraisal in Step 1 and the results of your '12 Ms' internal audit in Step 2 and bring these reflections together:

	Problems identified	Opportunities uncovered
Step 1: External appraisal (Temples)		
Step 2: Internal audit (12 Ms)		

STEP 3 SUMMARY

Step 3 helps to:

▮ Bring together reflections on information gathered from your 'Temples' and '12 Ms' tables;

▮ Summarise your analysis;

▮ Summarise your audit.

Step 4

Predicting where you are going

Will help you to:

■ Predict what will happen if you change nothing

■ Envisage the worst case scenario

PREDICTING WHERE YOU ARE GOING

The following *change nothing scenario* may help you to forecast where you will end up if you change nothing:

No	Area	If you change nothing . . .	Yes (✓)	No (✓)
1.	Problems	Does your organisation's current course of action overcome the problems identified in Step 3?		
2.	Market position	a) Does your organisation's current course of action exploit the opportunities uncovered in Step 3? b) Will you be able to maintain your market position (Step 2)?		
3.	Human resources	a) Will your current marketing, managerial and operational skills be enough to last you the next five to ten years (Step 2)? b) Is the organisation's current direction acceptable to employees (Step 2)?		
4.	Finance	a) Is your organisation's current course leading to satisfactory financial performance (Step 2)? b) Can the current course of action be funded over the next few years (Step 2)? c) Will the financial risks (eg, liquidity ratio) change for the better over the next five to ten years (Step 2)? d) Will your organisation's current course of action improve your organisation's capital structure over the next five to ten years (Step 2)? e) Will you be able to have the same relationship with your funding bodies over the next five to ten years (Step 2)?		

No	Area	If you change nothing ...	Yes (✓)	No (✓)
5.	Competitors	Will your competitors stay as they are over the next five to ten years (Step 2)?		
6.	Customers	a) Is your organisation capable of responding to any increased levels of service expectation from customers (Step 2)? b) Will you be able to have the same relationship with your customers over the next five to ten years (Step 2)? c) Will your organisation's current direction improve the quality of services or products over the next five to ten years (Step 2)?		
7.	Culture	Does the current direction of the organis-ation fit its culture (Step 2)?		
8.	Technology	Will your technology allow you to compete over the next five to ten years (Step 2)?		
9.	Raw materials	Will you be able to obtain the necessary raw materials over the next ten years (Step 2)?		
10.	Supplies	Will you be able to have the same relationship with your suppliers over the next five to ten years (Step 2)?		

Worst case scenario

Look back at the ten sets of questions in the *'change nothing scenario'*, and for each question you answered 'No', complete the following:

No	For each question answered 'No' what might be the implications in ten years' time of that answer? The worst case scenario might be:

STEP 4 SUMMARY

Step 4 will have helped you to:

▌ Predict what will happen if you change nothing

▌ Envisage the worst case scenario

Step 5

Deciding where you should be going

Will help you to:

▌ Formulate a mission statement

▌ Create a vision

▌ Determine a direction

▌ Agree some objectives

DECIDING WHERE TO GO

From Missions to Visions – Seeking a Strategic Direction

Firstly, try to answer the following questions:

- What do you sell or provide?
    - Products? How many different types and ranges?
    - Services? Who could benefit from them and how?

_____

_____

_____

_____

- What do you intend to sell or provide in the future?
    - Products? How many different types?
    - Services? Who could benefit from them and how?

_____

_____

_____

_____

- Why would people use *your* product or service rather others'?

_____

_____

_____

_____

■   Who are your customers?

- – Individual members of the public?

- – What social class and locality?

- – Manufacturing companies? What size, nature, area?

_____

_____

_____

_____

■   How do you reach your customers?

- – Passing trade, press advertisements, direct mail shots or through sales representatives or selling agencies?

_____

_____

_____

_____

■   How do you obtain products or supplies?

- – Manufacture from raw materials?

- – Assemble from intermediates?

_____

_____

_____

_____

▌ How do you provide your services?
 – Through partners, employees, contractors, franchisees?

_____

_____

_____

_____

▌ How do you sell to your customers?

 – Direct to the public, via manufacturers, through shops, using conventional or electronic mail?

_____

_____

_____

_____

▌ How do you support your sales or services?

 – How and where do you deliver?

_____

_____

_____

_____

Now try to draft a mission statement. At first it may fill a page as you go back over what it should contain and keep adding ingredients. Keep refining and polishing your statement until it is comprehensive and reads fluently. In its final form, it may be one or two long, complicated sentences, extending perhaps to half a page.

Later, you can extract certain 'strategic directions' or a 'vision', which you can encourage everyone to share. It may become the basis of a 'promise' or a 'charter' for your organisation.

Although 'strategic directions' and 'visions' can be derived from mission statements, they are no substitute for a well-thought out mission statement that attempts to encompass wider issues.

Refining a mission statement is an important step in your strategic planning process. The 'promises' or 'charters' for customers and the 'strategic directions' and 'visions' for your organisation that follow from this, may be needed during the implementation.

Once you have drafted your mission statement, circulate it as widely as possible for individual written comments. At the same time, encourage the draft to be used as a focus for discussions by teams and groups, at meetings called solely for that purpose. This can be a good way of giving feedback and thanks to people whom you identified as influential or well informed during your information gathering and strategic analysis in Steps 1, 2 and 3.

From Missions to Desirable Objectives

A voyage of a thousand miles begins with but a single step.
(Confucius – 600 BC)

Our theme of 'keep checking' reflects the iterative learning and thinking models that underlie our strategic planning process. Key people identified during Steps 1 and 2 can be revisited to check out the emerging mission statement. Information gaps may be filled. They may know about hazards and obstacles that lie in the way of your tentative or intended strategic directions. You are making allies and assessing resistances to your eventual implementation plans.

Similarly, in this next move, from key areas of the mission to an agreed set of objectives, you should cross-check your emerging ideas with the key people affected.

Complete the table on the following page. Inserted into the table are some key areas that are often worth considering.

Key Areas from the Mission Statement	Agreed Desirable Objectives
1. Growth	
Rate of sales growth?	
Rate of earnings growth?	
Increase in market share?	
Mergers and aquisitions?	
Expansion of the range of services?	
Disinvestments?	
2. Stability	
Utilisation of capacity?	
Fluctuation of earnings?	
3. Return	
Return on investment in business?	
4. Skills	
How much research and development?	
Percentage of managers and staff with vocational qualifications?	
5. Assets	
Replacements?	
Maintain, enhance value?	
6. Other objectives	
Collaborations, partnership arrangements?	
What about social responsibilities?	
How will you maintain or improve your organisation's status and reputation?	
How will you improve your public image?	
How will you increase employees' security?	
How will you work to maintain and improve employees' and customer welfare?	

Prompt Sheet on 'Creating a Vision' and Determining a 'Direction'

Strategic Vision,   Strategic Intent,   Desired State,

Overall Purpose

Above are some of the words that are used to describe a statement encapsulating what an organisation is about. It is often a statement about the organisation's business aims, its products and services and about what distinguishes its business from others, often in terms of cost, quality and reliability. The idea of making such a statement is to encapsulate the organisation's overall purpose, so that it may become widely understood and acted upon by the organisation's key stakeholders. Important stakeholders include customers, employees, suppliers, financiers and members of the community.

Among other gains, it is hoped that employees who 'own' the organisation's 'vision' and who are aware of its intended 'strategic direction', will feel more confident and more 'empowered' to take decisions that are consistent with the organisation's overall purpose.

The table opposite indicates some of the strategic issues to be addressed and the way in which a mission statement may help to orchestrate a debate about these issues among the organisation's stakeholders and other key people who were identified during the strategic analysis and information-gathering for Steps 1, 2 and 3.

Strategic issue to be debated	How drafting a mission statement might help
Unanimity of 'direction'	A mission statement should help people understand better where the organisation is trying to get to.
Market orientation	A mission statement should make clear who the customers are and what they need, want and can expect.
Organisational culture	A mission statement should embody the ethos of the organisation, espousing its values and beliefs, indicating 'how things are done and not done around here'.
Focus	A mission statement should help people to focus their efforts, empowering them to take decisions on their own authority, within the spirit of the mission.
Resource utilisation	A mission statement should help people to make more of their own decisions on priorities and the allocation or resources.
Motivation	A mission statement should embody that which is inspirational. Employees need to feel that the effort and time that they devote to their working lives is worthwhile.
A 'vision'	A mission statement should provide a means of thinking beyond today, a 'vision' of our inspirations for the future, embracing what we 'want' and 'ought' to do, as well as what we 'can' do.

How are the 'Mission' and the 'Vision' Related?

This relationship is based on one informing the other. The mission statement has more facets. The mission statement should:

■   clarify and limit the purpose of the organisation

■   indicate the nature of the business, its customers, its resources, its main activities, technologies and expertise, its position at the moment and where it wants to be

■   make clear who are the key people, or groups of people, inside and outside the organisation and how decisions are made. It should convey a sense of the organisation's history and its distinctiveness. (It might clarify the main 'opportunities' it is seeking to exploit and the main 'problems' it is seeking to circumvent)

■   convey the values of the organisation, helping to answer questions about 'the way we do things around here'.

The *vision* is hopefully an inspirational resonance of desires, values and possibilities, which overlap:

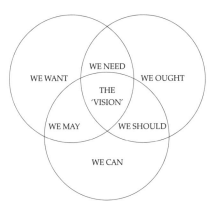

The 'vision' should be embedded in the 'mission'. The 'vision' should be realistic in the light of other facets of the mission.

Prompt Sheet on Agreeing
Desirable Strategic Objectives

Desirable strategic objectives are the long-term results that an organisation is seeking to achieve, in pursuit of its basic mission.

Many organisations have multiple objectives. The abilities and preferences of its managers often influence the choice of these objectives.

An organisation's objectives need to be related to its mission and hence to its 'vision' and 'strategic direction':

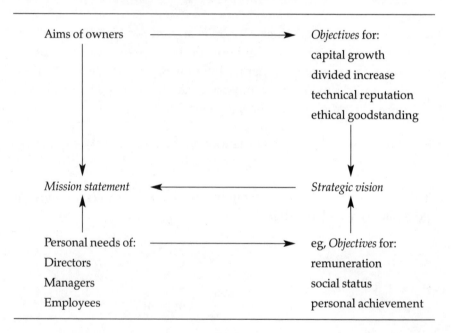

Aims of owners ──────────▶ *Objectives* for:

capital growth

divided increase

technical reputation

ethical goodstanding

Mission statement ◀────────── *Strategic vision*

Personal needs of: ──────────▶ eg, *Objectives* for:

Directors — remuneration

Managers — social status

Employees — personal achievement

Here are some examples of desirable strategic objectives:

Directional objectives	Examples
Market leadership	Competitive ranking; rate of innovation; new patents; market share; licensing deals.
Market spread	Number of different markets; number of customer groups; number of industries.
Performance objectives	
Growth	Increases in sales, profit, capital.
Investment	Return on capital; return on assets.
Profitability	Margin on sales; earnings per share.
Internal objectives	
Efficiency	Ratio of sales to assets; sales to stock.
Personnel	Employee relations; morale; staff development; average employee pay; retention; levels of skill.
External objectives	
Social responsibility	Public relations; percentage recycled; community involvement; emissions; miles travelled by staff, suppliers. Charitable donations, endowments.

(Adapted from Greenley, GE (1986) *The Strategic and Operational Planning of Marketing*, p 51, McGraw-Hill Ltd)

What are useful characteristics of desirable strategic objectives?

■ Realistic – they seem achievable within the required timescales.

■ Communicable – it is easy to get others to understand them.

■ Measurable – it is always possible to answer the question, 'How will we know when we have achieved them?' This does not always require the measure to be a quantity. Often, very visible qualitative measures can be more effective than detailed statistics.

■ Relevant – it is possible to see how their achievement will make a major contribution to the fulfilment of the organisation's 'vision' and the pursuit of its 'mission'. The relationship may be illustrated as:

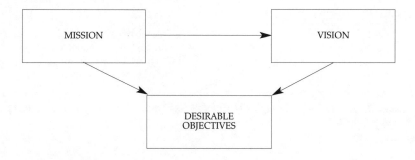

On the next page is an example of how one organisation agreed a set of desirable objectives.

An example of how one company derived its desirable strategic objectives from its mission statement.

The following key statements were extracted from the Mission Statement of Streatham Piping:

- To provide products and services for the monitoring, operation and maintenance of essential piping systems.

- To sustain profitable growth sufficient to meet the needs of the stakeholders in the business (suppliers, employees, community, customers, family and other shareholders).

- To remain a private, family controlled company.

- Growth to be achieved primarily by expanding activities in areas related to existing businesses.

- To maintain a position of leadership and integrity in business as perceived by customers, employees and the community.

(Adapted from a case reported in *Long Range Planning*, 1991, Vol 24, Bates, D L and Dillard, J E, 'Desired future position – a practical tool for planning', p 97, with permission from Elsevier Science Ltd, The Boulevard, Lansford Lane, Kidlington OX5 1GB.)

Arising out of Streatham's Mission Statement, possible key areas for objective setting are:			
	A focus could be on ...	*A level could be ...*	*Tentative Desirable Strategic Objectives to be offered for adoption*
'Profitable growth in related businesses'	Existing products	50 million p.a. sales	to have 50 million p.a. sales, from existing products, by 2010.
	New products	10 million p.a. sales	to have 10 million p.a. sales, from new products by 2010.
	Business acquisitions	20 million p.a. sales	to have 20 million p.a. sales from business acquisitions, by 2010.
'Leadership'	International sales	25 million p.a. sales	to have 25 million p.a. international sales, by 2010.
	Plastic pipe construction	to become a full line producer	to have 100% of API standard plastic pipe connections produced by own facilities, by 2010.
'Integrity'	Quality	no more than 0.5% rejects	to have no more than 0.5% internal rejects, by 2010.
	Quality	100% meet standards	to have 100% of shipped products meet internal standards, by 2010.
To be 'market driven'	Customer requests or problems	immediate underwater testing and repair	to have in place an operation that provides immediate underwater testing and repair of pipelines, by 2010.
	Service level	24 hour delivery world-wide	to provide 24 hour world-wide delivery from four service centres, by 2010.

Tentative Desirable Strategic Objectives for next fifteen years

These 'Tentative Desirable Strategic Objectives' were considered by the Streatham Management Board. They rejected them! The process of rejection and modification of their desirable objectives helped them to clarify their 'vision' for their company. This caused them to revisit their draft mission statement. They made a few changes and then decided that they would return to their mission statement after they had considered what long-term options might be open to them, ie, after they had completed Steps 6 and 7.

Now use your mission statement to orchestrate a debate about desirable long-term objectives, using the table below to help you.

Arising out of your mission statement			
Possible key areas for objective setting are:	A focus could be on:	A level could be:	Tentative desirable strategic objectives to be offered for adoption

For adoption as desirable strategic objectives for the next – years

You now have more idea about what your organisation wants to achieve and maybe what it ought to achieve. You also have more knowledge about the world in which these achievements must be won and what your competitors might do to try to stop you. In the next two steps of your strategic planning you can use this knowledge to help you to generate some strategic options. Finally, you will evaluate these options, select some and then set about planning their implementation.

STEP 5 SUMMARY

Step 5 will have helped you to:

▌ Formulate a mission statement

▌ Create a vision

▌ Determine a direction

▌ Agree some objectives

Step 6

Minding
the gaps

Will help you to:

▌ Identify obstacles to achieving
your objectives

▌ Assess whether they are
removable

▌ Modify your objectives

MIND THE GAPS

Complete the table on the next page:

1. Across the top, enter your organisation's Agreed Desirable Objectives from Step 5.

2. Down the left-hand column, enter forecasts for any relevant factor identified in Step 4.

3. Compare each forecast against each objective.

4. Enter an 'X' if the comparison reveals an obstacle.

5. Identify the strategic changes needed to remove obstacles to the achievement of Desirable Strategic Objectives. Almost certainly more strategic options will be needed and the removal of obstacles might require even more creative thinking. This will then take you briskly on to Step 7.

(There is a worked example of how this obstacle analysis was carried out by Streatham Piping.)

Gap Analysis

	Desirable strategic objectives (Step 5)			
Based on Step 4, what was your forecast in relation to ...				
1. Problems?				
2. Market position?				
3. Human resources?				
4. Finances?				
5. Competitors?				

Gap analysis (continued)

	Desirable strategic objectives (Step 5)			
Based on Step 4, what was your forecast in relation to ...				
6. Customers?				
7. Culture?				
8. Technology?				
9. Raw materials?				
10. Suppliers?				

Streatham Piping's Gap Analysis

This worked example shows how Streatham Piping compared their forecast of where they were going (Step 4) with some of their Desirable Strategic Objectives (Step 5).

	Specimen desirable objectives (based on Step 5)		
When Streatham completed Step 4, their forecasts were …	*10 million p.a. sales from new products by 2010*	*25 million p.a. international sales by 2010*	*100% API pipe connections made by us*
1. Problems a. Over-capacity in industry b. Competitors' market power c. Over-wide product range d. Poor information systems	X	X	X
2. Market position a. Forecast to be in 'shake-out'			
3. Human resources a. Many tiers of management b. Poor management skills at shop-floor level	X	X	X
4. Finances a. Good relations with bank b. Seasonal cash flow	X	X	X
5. Competitors a. International market place b. Maturing market			
6. Customers a. Quality of goods b. Poor quality of after service	X	X	X

	Specimen desirable objectives (based on Step 5)		
When Streatham completed Step 4, their forecasts were …	*10 million p.a. sales from new products by 2010*	*25 million p.a. international sales by 2010*	*100% API pipe connections made by us*
7. Culture a Innovative b. Hard core of resistant managers		X	X
8. Technology a. Limited information systems b Modern office equipment	X	X	X
9. Raw materials a. New synthetic plastics b. Increasing fuel prices			
10. Suppliers a. Good relations with plastic industry and research establishments			

X = Obstacle to the feasibility of a particular objective

Identifying Strategic Changes Needed to Remove Obstacles or to Modify Objectives

Obstacle (identified by X)	The objective threatened	Removable? Yes/No	If yes, how?	If no, modified Desirable Objective is ...

Leading to a list of objectives that are both feasible and desirable, with an indication of the actions needed to remove the obstacles.

You have now completed the first six steps of your Nine Step Strategic Planning Cycle. In terms of our initial framework, you have gathered information for your strategic analysis and formulated ideas about your strategic direction. Having modified your desirable objectives to make sure they contribute to your mission and having avoided some insuperable obstacles, you are clearer about what it is that you want your strategic thinking to achieve. The last three steps are concerned with how to achieve this, ie, with planning action.

STEP 6 SUMMARY

Step 6 will have helped you to:

■ Identify obstacles to achieving your objectives

■ Assess whether they are removable

■ Modify your objectives

Step 7

Creating more options

Will help you to:

▎ Analyse existing options

▎ Create new options

▎ Consider all options

CREATING MORE OPTIONS

Now that you are clearer about what you wish your organisation to achieve, it is time to consider your options.

The strategic options on the following page are elaborated in the prompt sheets. If you would like some help on how to come up with new ideas, turn to the prompt sheets on creative thinking.

Once you have so many options that you need to become selective, you are probably ready for Step 8, in which you will be able to evaluate each option, using six strategic criteria. You will then be able to see which of the options you generated during this step, Step 7, will best achieve the desirable objectives that you established during Step 6. In the final step, Step 9, you will plan the implementation of the options you will have selected during Step 8.

Identifying Strategic Options

Strategic options	What might you gain from this option?	What are the problems with this option?	Examples of this option
Change nothing			
Concentration			
Product development			
Market development			
Innovation			
Horizontal integration			
Vertical integration			
Concentric diversification			
Retrenchment			
Turnaround			
Divestment			
Liquidation			

Prompt Sheet on Strategic Options

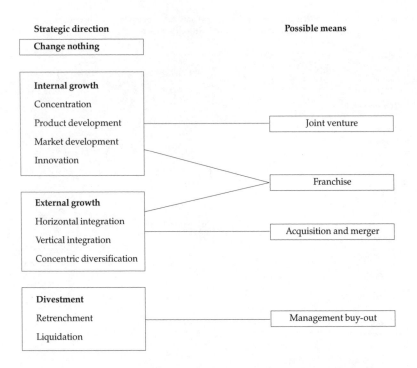

(Developed with permission from Thompson, J L (1990) *Strategic Management: Awareness & Change,* p 430, Figure17.1 'Strategic alternatives', Chapman & Hall.)

Change nothing

The 'change nothing' option is the one in which your organisation continues to follow, in broad terms, its current direction. As most organisations are confronting both internal and external changes, this option is sometimes not a good one to follow in the long term, but since the disruptive costs of change can be very high, the 'change nothing' scenario should always be considered seriously. In any event it provides a common point of comparison for other options.

Strategies for internal growth include:

Concentration
Resources can be focused towards the continued and profitable growth of a 'single' product or service in a 'single' market. This can be achieved by attracting new customers or by increasing their usage rate, or, where feasible, by attracting customers away from competitors. The advantage of this approach is that it uses the current skills in the organisation. Growth is not likely to be dramatic.

Product Development
An organisation can think about what modified products or services it could offer to its existing customers. This is generally less risky than trying to find new customers for existing products or services.

Market Development
An organisation can build on its existing strengths, skills and capabilities in order to market its present products or services to new customers, in related market areas. This often involves a new or renewed approaches to advertising, promotion and selling.

Innovation
This implies the development of products or services that are new, as opposed to modified. Innovative organisations can keep ahead of their competitors by introducing new products or services. Constant innovation requires new finance. If the new products will need to be sold to new customers, the risks associated with the new product's development will rise markedly.

Strategies for external growth include:

Horizontal Integration

This is integration that occurs when an organisation acquires or merges with a major competitor. Market share should increase and the organisation should be looking for situations in which the pooled skills and resources can generate a synergistic effect. These will be situations in which combined efforts should produce results that are greater than the mere arithmetic addition of previous market shares.

Vertical Integration

This is integration that occurs when an organisation acquires one of its suppliers or one of its customers. In this case the benefits looked for are not primarily in market share. Efficiency gains are sought through either better prices and delivery of components or through a better planned pattern of demand.

Concentric Diversification

Here the aim is to utilise the current marketing and research skills for one product or service, in order to develop a different or new product or service in another market. What is being sought here is a wider market for your organisation's knowledge, expertise or skill in carrying out certain processes, eg, research and development or product testing.

Strategies for divestment include:

Retrenchment
This may be required when an organisation experiences declining profits as a result of economic recession, production or service inefficiency, or through the activities of competitors that are innovating faster than it is. In these circumstances, the organisation will need to concentrate only on activities in which it has distinctive competencies. The aim is to reduce its operations to those in which the organisation has advantages over its competitors. Ideally, it will have further strategies to sustain those advantages in the face of anticipated changes and the actions likely to be taken by its competitors.

If an organisation fails to recover, there may be a need to sell off (or divest) part of the business. A management buy-out can be one way to do this. It is often associated with the need to raise finance, or is prompted when one part of the organisation is dragging down the rest.

Liquidation
This approach involves the sale of a complete business, either as a going concern or on a piecemeal basis. This may not necessarily be an admission of failure. It will sometimes be in the best interests, in the long term, of the stakeholders.

Prompt Sheet on Techniques to Aid Creativity

Everyone is creative. Some people can access their creativity more easily than others. Rapid change forces managers to think about the need for creativity and innovation in their organisations. Certain conditions can benefit this process:

■ Providing copious facilities
   for writing, drawing and display. Unrecorded ideas get lost easily

■ Using secluded locations
   helps to produce freedom from distractions

■ Setting tight time limits
   helps to prevent over-elaboration and inhibits evaluation

■ Raising energy
   creativity works best when people are aroused and enthusiastic.

1. Attribute Listing

This is a very simple method and is most useful when managers might be looking for the development of basic ideas, such as spin-offs from existing products or services:

A. Identify and pick out the major attributes of a product or service.

B. Suggest as many variations of each attribute as possible. Each combination of variations creates a potentially different product, service or idea.

C. List all the combinations. Evaluate them later.

As an example, consider you have been employed as a consultant by a Christmas novelty company to come up with new ideas for balloons. After discussions with the company, you decide that the major attributes for the novelty balloons are: colour; size; shape; price; durability. Using the above A, B, C approach:

A – *Major attributes*; we could have:
size, shape, price, durability.

B – *Possible variations*; we could have:
colours – red, purple, polka-dot, etc
size – 1 cm, 1 metre, 3 metres
shape – banana, star
price – 10p each, £1 each, £25 each
durability – 5 minutes, 1 year, 10-year guarantee

C – *Possible combinations*; we could have:
3-metre polka-dot banana, £25, ten-year guarantee.

(Adapted from Cooke and Slack (1991) *Making Management Decisions*, 2nd edn, by permission of the publisher, Prentice Hall International, Hemel Hempstead.)

You would then need to decide which of the potential products you think might be worth taking further as possible new balloon products.

2. Brainstorming

This is useful in tackling 'how to do' problems, or those where a new broad idea or direction is needed. The process involves presenting the problem or the opportunity and then generating as many ideas as possible, in a limited time, preferably using a large (6 to 16) group of people.

Every possible idea is recorded in a way that everyone can see. Flipcharts are commonly used. Someone usually keeps a note of all suggestions and feeds them through to the flipchart in a steady stream, acting as a kind of reservoir or 'header tank' of ideas, so as to keep the flow of ideas going. Zany ideas are encouraged, as is humour. Such ideas may be 'planted' in the audience to create a permissive atmosphere. Negativism, realism, scepticism and in particular cynicism are not allowed and must be quickly squashed by the person facilitating the brainstorming sessions. Pauses are filled by reading back the ideas already recorded on the flipcharts. The flipcharts should be torn off and displayed around the room. Ideas can be short-listed and evaluated later, using some of the techniques described in Step 8.

3. Forced relationships

This is based on the establishment of new relationships between normally unrelated objects or ideas. In a forced linking process, new applications are sought for existing products or services. One object is fixed; the other is chosen at random.

You then have to find as many ways as possible to relate the fixed object to the one chosen at random. As an example, consider you are a manager of a doctors' surgery with, say, six doctors. The declining number of patients on your surgery list has placed your future as a large practice in jeopardy. Your workforce is highly skilled and flexible. You have been asked to think up new ideas for diversifying your services. First you brainstorm list A – a list of all the things your staff can do, for example:

Possible services

A1. Medical diagnosis

A2. Minor surgery

A3. Health education

A4. Blood tests

A5. Bed baths, etc.

Tear the lists into strips and put them in a hat. Next you brainstorm list B – a list of possible areas in which you could provide services, for example:

Possible areas

B1. Schools

B2. Houses

B3. Insurance companies

B4. Football clubs

B5. Supermarkets

B6. Chemists

B7. Charities.

Again, tear the list into strips and put them in a separate hat. Next you draw one strip from each hat and in five minutes you have to write down as many uses as possible for the service chosen from list A, eg, medical diagnosis, in the area chosen from list B.

Prompt Sheet on Considering Strategic Options

A choice between the options in your table may not be a real choice. A particular strategy is only an option if it could be implemented. A number of factors will need to be considered:

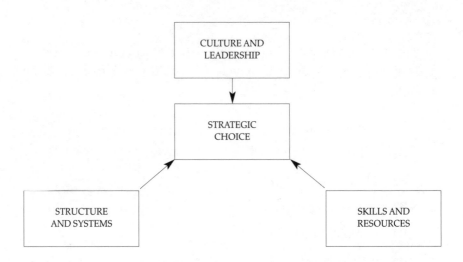

Consider the external appraisal in Step 1 and the opportunities that are present for your organisation. If they fall within the organisation's mission, they will affect your decision. Then consider the internal audit that you did in Step 2 and any opportunities or abilities to obtain resources that it revealed. On the other side of the coin, discovered problems, either internally or externally, may well constrain your choice. Your personal aspirations will also influence your choice. This is demonstrated in the figure on the next page:

(Figure adapted from Bowman (1990), *The Essence of Strategic Management,* by permission of the publisher, Prentice Hall International, Hemel Hempstead.)

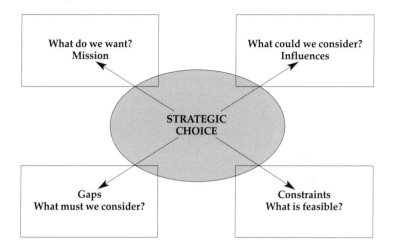

STEP 7 SUMMARY

Step 7 will have helped you to:

▊ Analyse existing options

▊ Create new options

▊ Consider all options

Step 8

Checking them for sense

Will help you to assess the relative:

- competitiveness
- controllability
- compatibility
- feasibility
- impact
- risk

of each of your options

CHECKING THEM FOR SENSE

You may be considering options, the likely consequences of which are beyond your experience or partly out of your control. You may need to accept a trade-off between control over the consequences of the option and the potential contribution the option might make to your mission and objectives.

Complete the following table by rating each option either A, B or C for each of the six evaluation criteria, where A is a high rating, C is a poor rating and B is somewhere in between. (If you would like help in arriving at your ABC ratings, you could turn to the prompt sheets.

First devise a brief description, or label, for each of your options (see Step 7) and enter the labels in the table.

Six evaluation criteria How would you assess each option for:	Change nothing	Option 1 (label)	Option 2 (label)	Option 3 (label)	Option 4 (label)	Option 5 (label)
Competitiveness						
Controllability						
Compatibility						
Feasibility						
Impact						
Risk						
Total number of As						

In order to draw up a shortlist of options for further consideration, start by eliminating any option that has a C rating against any of the evaluation criteria. Then give further consideration to those options that have the highest number of A ratings; these would appear to be the most likely candidates for your strategic choice. Compare what would happen if your organisation adopted them, with the 'change nothing' option. To what extent do these options help to fill the gap between where your organisation is now and where you have identified you want to be (Step 5)? Do you have sufficient strategic options? Not all options are likely to be implemented on time and not all options will deliver 100 per cent of your expectations. Do you need a safety margin? Can you over-provide now and, if necessary, prune later?

Prompt Sheet on Evaluating Options

Evaluation is simply putting a value on something. In order to put a value on an option, you need to understand and describe what will happen if you decide to pursue it. One way to evaluate options is to rate them, giving either an A, B or C rating, depending on how well they meet certain conditions or criteria.

What exactly should you evaluate?

For each option, you need to consider:

- ▪ *competitiveness*
- ▪ *controllability*
- ▪ *compatibility*

- ▪ *feasibility*
- ▪ *impact*
- ▪ *risk.*

This is summarised in the figure below:

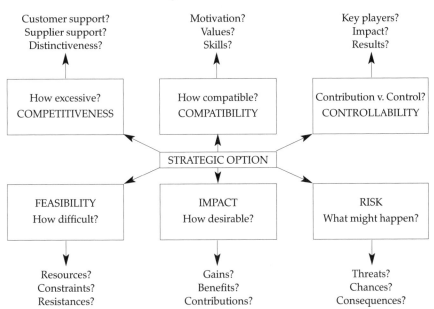

To assess the *competitiveness* of an option, you need to identify how exclusively you are able to deliver this option when compared with your potential competitors. Will your organisation stand out against the competition?

To assess the *compatibility* of an option, you will need to weigh up the team's skills, knowledge and motivation, to ensure that the option 'fits' with the organisation's resources and morale. Technical or professional skills and knowledge may be needed, in addition to skills and knowledge of how to work together as a team.

To assess the *controllability* that an organisation has over an option, you will need to assess the balance between the amount of control the organisation normally requires, and the extent to which the contribution of the option to the mission could really be controlled.

The *feasibility* of an option indicates the ease with which the option could be implemented. You will need to think about the time, effort and money involved.

The *impact* of an option is the extent to which it would impact on, or contribute to, the organisation's mission and objectives.

To assess the *risks* of an option, you will need to think about the kind of things that could go wrong, the chances that they might go wrong and the extent of the consequences if they did go wrong.

Evaluating competitiveness

For an option to be successful, there is often a need for it to be special or unique, or at least readily distinguishable from what your competitors are already offering. An organisation also needs to know whether its potential major customers and suppliers of raw materials would also support this option. Without this support, the chances of the option succeeding may be very limited.

In the summary table enter:

A   if the option would be highly competitive with what your competitors might offer;

B   if the option is likely to be reasonably competitive;

C   if the option is merely comparable to or only marginally different from that which your competitors might offer.

Evaluating compatibility

Organisations are not composed of totally like-minded people. They may have differing professional or technical skills, different professional or cultural values, interests or experiences. Differences in values and skills can cause problems in assessing whether an option is compatible with the team of people who would be involved with a particular option. Would a shortage of particular skills cause problems when implementing this option? If so, can these be bought in, or is there a local or indeed a national shortage? Is the team likely to be sufficiently motivated to adapt, and implement successfully, this option? What might be in it for them? Who would be the key players, influencers and change agents? How would they be likely to react to this option?

In the summary table enter:

A   if there is a readily identifiable team who would embrace this option with skill and enthusiasm;
B   if you could identify a few key players who would make a competent job of assembling a project team for this option;
C   if there are major and chronic skill deficiencies or if the option would pose a major clash of values or interests.

Evaluating controllability

With some options, it is possible to see clearly that if they succeed they will have a highly beneficial impact and may make a significant contribution to the overall mission and objectives of the organisation. However, it may be difficult for the organisation to control, say, the likelihood of success, the exact extent of the benefits or the timing of their impact. Some organisations can tolerate different degrees of uncertainty or lack of control. This may be for historical, cultural or financial reasons. In any event, there will need to be a reasonable match between the degree of control normally required by the organisation and that which is possible with the strategic options that are finally chosen.

For example, suppose an option is to merge with a competitor. The evaluation shows that the impact on sales is likely to be very good because of certain synergies that will be created by the merger. But the merger will involve reorganising two companies. This will be complicated, involving many people who may not agree with or understand the purpose of the merger. The organisation can try to educate, inform and motivate, but the fact remains that while it would be reasonable to hope for and perhaps expect increased sales performance, its achievement is substantially out of the organisation's control. In this case, although the organisation knows clearly that the key result is sales, which are relatively easy to monitor, many of the key players are unknown and the means to control their performance may not be in place.

In the summary table enter:

A   if the achievement of the contribution to the organisation's mission and objectives is highly controllable;
B   if the organisation is likely to be able to exercise sufficient control to ensure a worthwhile level of contribution to the organisation's mission and objectives;
C   if the extent of the potential beneficial impact cannot be easily estimated nor its achievement controlled.

Evaluating feasibility

At least three areas should be considered: resources, constraints and resistances.

All strategic options will require some kind of *resourcing*, even if it is a retrenchment, a disposal or a de-merger. Time will be needed: whose and is it likely to be available? Expertise will probably be needed: does your organisation have it, does it know where to get it or know someone who will? Will your organisation need new or extra raw materials, new suppliers? More money for working capital or to create extra space or new packaging?

Does your organisation have the technology, is it sufficiently up to date and is there enough capacity? Will the option generate a need for more control information? Can existing information systems handle this or does your organisation need more or faster information processing capacity?

Even if your organisation has, or can easily obtain, the resources, there will be *constraints* on how your organisation uses them: legal, procedural, health and safety, environmental, ethical, social, energy, waste disposal, agreements on working practices, professional, national and international standards, embargoes, quotas, export and other licences, lending limits, borrowing limits and other values and cultural constraints that may be enshrined in your organisation's mission.

Even if the options can be resourced and could be implemented within the constraints within which your organisation must work, your option will require the agreement of some and preferably the active cooperation of many people in the organisation. Some *resistance*, from some people, can usually be managed as part of the change process, but widespread, strongly maintained resistance, especially from key players, decision-makers and influencers, will greatly reduce the feasibility of the option.

In the summary table enter:

A   if the option is going to be easy;
B   if the option is going to be difficult;
C   if the option is almost impossible.

Evaluating impact

The impact of an option is the extent to which it furthers the mission and contributes to the objectives of the organisation. How desirable is its impact likely to be on the organisation's:

■   outputs;

■   finances;

■   learning;

■   reputation;

■   culture and values?

Re-read your organisation's draft mission statement (Step 5) and ask yourself to what extent this option will contribute. Do you think it is essential, desirable or only marginal in its likely contribution?

In the summary table enter:

A   if the option is an essential contribution;
B   if the option is a desirable contribution;
C   if the option is only a marginal contribution.

Evaluating risks

Would only a small error in the assumptions involved in this option produce consequences that might be catastrophic for the organisation? If so, the option may be too high a risk. Re-read your external appraisal (Step 1). Are there risks associated with possible changes in:

Technology;   Economy;   Markets;   Politics;   Law;
Ethics;   Society?

And what would be the consequences for your organisation if these 'TEMPLES' changes occurred? For each possible change, consider:

Case I – you pursue the option.

Case II – you do not pursue the option.

Finally, and all important, how are your competitors likely to react if you do, or do not, pursue this option? The risks and consequences of not pursuing a particular option are sometimes worse than if you pursue it! Is pursuing the option the least worst case?

In the summary table enter:

A   if the option carries low risk;
B   if the option carries moderate risk with manageable
    consequences;
C   if the option carries unreasonable risks that threaten the
    survival of the organisation.

Additional Prompt Sheet on Rating Your Options for Competitiveness

For each option, consider the following six questions on its competitiveness. Depending on your answer, allocate a score out of the number shown against the question:

The six questions	Change nothing	Option 1 (label)	Option 2 (label)	Option 3 (label)
How special or distinctive are the products you intend to sell or the services you intend to provide?	/35	/35	/35	/35
How sure are you that you can deliver the distinctiveness of the goods or services?	/25	/25	/25	/25
How timely is it to start providing these goods or services?	/5	/5	/5	/5
How easy will it be to advertise your products or services?	/20	/20	/20	/20
How well do you know your competitors and the products or services they are providing?	/25	/25	/25	/25
How supportive are the major potential customers for the intended new products or services?	/40	/40	/40	/40
Total score (out of 150)	/150	/150	/150	/150

If an option scores 100 or more, give it an A for competitiveness.

If an option scores 75 or less, give it a C for competitiveness.

Otherwise give the option a B rating.

Then transfer the ratings to the summary table.

Additional Prompt Sheet on Rating Your Options for Compatibility

For each option, consider the following six questions about your organisation, or the team that would need to implement the option. Depending on your answer, allocate a score out of the number shown against the question. For example, when you have considered the question about team motivation, give the team a score out of 50. The next question about technical skills requires a score out of 10 (this is because missing technical skills can be more easily purchased than motivation!):

The six questions	Change nothing	Option 1 (label)	Option 2 (label)	Option 3 (label)
Do you and your team have the motivation for this option?	/50	/50	/50	/50
Do you and your team have the technical skills for this option?	/10	/10	/10	/10
Do you and your team have the skills needed to look after the administration of this option?	/15	/15	/15	/15
Have you the ability to sell or promote these goods or services?	/30	/30	/30	/30
Are you confident that you will be able to manage the time?	/25	/25	/25	/25
Are working conditions, wages, etc, adequate to retain and attract the kind of staff you will need?	/20	/20	/20	/20
Total score (out of 150)	/150	/150	/150	/150

If an option scores 100 or more, give it an A for compatibility.

If an option scores 75 or less, give it a C for compatibility.

Otherwise give the option a B rating.

Then transfer the ratings to the summary table.

Additional Prompt Sheet on Rating Your Options for Controllability

Try to complete one of the priority matrices opposite for each of your options. This involves assessing the degree of control the organisation has over each option, and the impact the option might have on your organisation's mission and objectives. Fill in a table like the one opposite for each option you are considering by circling the letter in the box that you think best describes each option, where:

A = high control over beneficial impact.
B = reasonable control over beneficial impact.
C = uncertain control over beneficial impact.

Enter label of selected option: eg, 'change nothing'	Beneficial impact on mission and objectives		
	Low	*Medium*	*High*
Degree of your control over likely success			
Largely under control	C	B	A
Partially under control	C	C	B
Little or no control	C	C	C

Enter label of selected option:	Beneficial impact on mission and objectives		
	Low	*Medium*	*High*
Degree of your control over likely success			
Largely under control	C	B	A
Partially under control	C	C	B
Little or no control	C	C	C

Enter label of selected option:	Beneficial impact on mission and objectives		
	Low	*Medium*	*High*
Degree of your control over likely success			
Largely under control	C	B	A
Partially under control	C	C	B
Little or no control	C	C	C

Now transfer the circled letters for each option to the summary table.

Additional Prompt Sheet on Rating Your Options for Feasibility

For each option, consider the following eight questions. Depending on your answer, allocate a score out of the number shown:

Reconsidering Steps 1, 2 and 6 ...	Change nothing	Option 1 (label)	Option 2 (label)	Option 3 (label)
How easy will it be to raise the funds for this option?	/35	/35	/35	/35
How easy will it be to achieve the share of the market that will be needed?	/35	/35	/35	/35
To what extent do you already have the managerial skills that you will need?	/15	/15	/15	/15
How easy will it be to aquire any missing skills?	/15	/15	/15	/15
How easy will it be to aquire technology?	/10	/10	/10	/10
How easy will it be to aquire the services and raw materials?	/10	/10	/10	/10
How easy will it be to cover the outgoing cash flow, and interest payments?	/25	/25	/25	/25
How well does this option fit the organisation's culture?	/10	/10	/10	/10
Total score (out of 150)	/150	/150	/150	/150

If an option scores 100 or more, give it an A for feasibility.

If an option scores 75 or less, give it a C for feasibility.

Otherwise give the option a B rating.

Then transfer the ratings to the summary table.

Additional Prompt Sheet on Rating Your Options for Impact

For each option, consider the following six questions. Depending on your answer, allocate a score out of the number shown against the question:

The six questions:	Change nothing	Option 1 *(label)*	Option 2 *(label)*	Option 3 *(label)*
To what extent would this option make your organisation more profitable or enable you to provide more benefits for the same cost?	/30	/30	/30	/30
To what extent would your liquidity ratio change for the better?	/20	/20	/20	/20
To what extent will the option improve quality?	/20	/20	/20	/20
To what extent will the option provide an edge over your competitors?	/30	/30	/30	/30
To what extent does the option exploit the opportunities in Step 3?	/10	/10	/10	/10
To what extent does the option contribute to the objectives in Step 5?	/40	/40	/40	/40
Total score (out of 150)	/150	/150	/150	/150

If an option scores 100 or more, give it an A for impact.

If an option scores 75 or less, give it a C for impact.

Otherwise give the option a B rating.

Then transfer the ratings to the summary table.

Additional Prompt Sheet on Rating Your Options for Risk

It might help your risk assessment if you try to complete, as best as you can, the table below:

Consider possible changes in...	Then estimate	Change nothing	Option 1 (label)	Option 2 (label)	Option 3 (label)
Technology	Chances				
	Consequences				
	Risk Assessment				
Economy	Chances				
	Consequences				
	Risk Assessment				
Markets	Chances				
	Consequences				
	Risk Assessment				
Politics	Chances				
	Consequences				
	Risk Assessment				
Law	Chances				
	Consequences				
	Risk Assessment				
Ethics	Chances				
	Consequences				
	Risk Assessment				
Society	Chances				
	Consequences				
	Risk Assessment				

Details of how to complete the above table can be found on the opposite page.

For each of your options, consider any threatening changes that might occur during the likely lifetime of the project. First, how do you rate the 'chances' of these threatening changes occurring? If there is an unlikely or small chance, enter an A in the chance column. If there is a possible chance, enter B. If there is a likely or probable chance, enter C.

Next, consider the possible consequences for you, or your organisation, if you pursued the option and the threatening change *did* occur. If the consequences for your organisation would be inconvenient, but minor and manageable, enter A under consequences. If the consequences would be major, but surmountable within two or three years, enter B. If the consequences would threaten the survival of the organisation, enter C.

Now use the key below to record an overall assessment of risk against each of your options in the previous table by entering either A, B or C in the rows headed 'Risk Assessment' in the table on the previous page.

Key for risk assessment grading

When chance x consequences =	AA	AB	AC	BA	BB	BC	CA	CB	CC
Then overall Risk Assessment =	A	B	C	A	C	C	B	C	C

Now transfer an overall assessment of the risk of each option into the summary table. To do this proceed as follows:

If any option shows a C level of risk under any of the 'TEMPLES' headings, record C in the summary table.

If any option shows only As under its 'TEMPLES' headings, then the overall level to be recorded in the summary table is A.

If any option shows a combination of As and Bs under its 'TEMPLES' headings, record B in the summary table.

STEP 8 SUMMARY

Step 8 will have helped you to assess the relative:

■ competitiveness

■ controllability

■ compatibility

■ feasibility

■ impact

■ risk

of each of your options

(Elements of Step 8 have developed ideas that first appeared in Cooke and Slack, (1991) *Making Management Decisions*, 2nd edn, and that have been used with the permission of the publisher, Prentice Hall International, Hemel Hempstead.)

Step 9

Deciding how to implement

Will help you to:

▌ Agree an action plan

▌ Decide how to reward progress

▌ Decide how to monitor progress

DECIDING HOW TO IMPLEMENT

Who's doing what by when? How will you know?
Targets, Action lists, Timescales, Resources needed

This book is concerned only with thinking about strategy.

When trying to complete Step 9 of your strategic thinking, it might be useful to anticipate what can be involved in managing the practical tasks involved in implementing strategy. There are companion books on *Implementing Changes* by Horne and Doherty (Routledge, 2000) and *Thinking Skills* by Wootton and Horne (Kogan Page, 2000), which address the practical problems of managing strategic change.

Identifying the key people

Review your notes from Step 1 (TEMPLES) and especially Step 2 (the 12 Ms). Brainstorm a list of the key people and decision-makers that you came across during the first eight steps. Any of these might have an interest in the plans you now wish to implement. In order to identify these stakeholders or key players, ask yourself the following questions:

▌ Who will be affected?

▌ Who could stop the implementation?

▌ Who could slow the implementation?

▌ Who could ease the implementation?

▌ What are their strengths and weaknesses?

▌ What interests them, outside as well as inside work?

▌ Would they welcome a challenging opportunity?

▌ Do they want to develop themselves?

▌ Have objectives and targets been agreed with them?

▌ Have you covered everyone to whom the mission statement refers?

How will you reward these people?

▌ Will your reward systems focus on groups or on individuals?

▌ Will you reward effort, capability, intentions or results?

▌ Will your rewards be financial, promotion or increased status?

▌ What sanctions might you need if people are not performing?

▌ Do your staff require new skills to implement the changes?

▌ If yes, how do you intend to develop these?

▌ What timescale do you envisage?

Control – how will you know what is happening?

■ Can you identify who will be responsible for what?

- Who will agree objectives with staff?

- Who will monitor them?

- Who will review them?

■ What are the key factors or key result areas?

■ How will you monitor them?

- What quantitative measures will you use?

- What qualitative measures will you use?

Managing the Timescales – using Gantt Charts

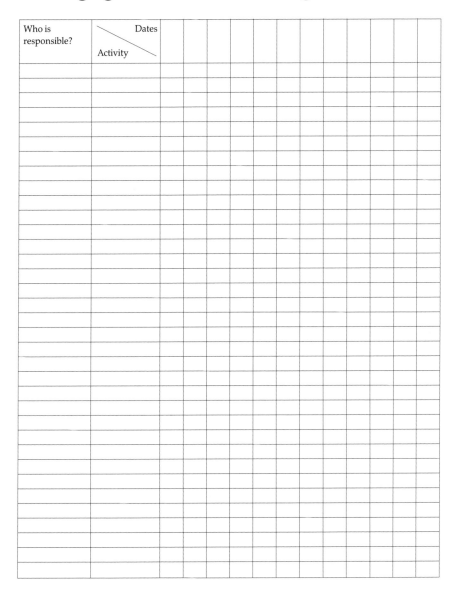

Who is responsible?	Activity	Dates													

If you are not familiar with Gantt charts, turn to the prompt sheet.

Monitoring Action Plans

Key task:

Person responsible:

Review of 'tight tolerances' (those for which careful monitoring is required as they are crucial to the implementation process and could jeopardise it):

If 'tight tolerance' is exceeded, what are the likely effects:

What are our options now?

What are the knock-on effects?

Proposed changes to implementation plan?

Date and time of next
monitoring meeting

Monitoring – Agreeing an Action Plan

Key person	Objectives agreed	Reward system agreed (if any)	Training required, when and how	Date of next review

Keep a file on each key person. The file should be updated with emerging information on that person's interests and motivation.

Enter the name of each key person into the table on the previous page and use the table to keep notes of the objectives you agree with them, any training needed and any reward systems that you have promised. The table should be used to structure an agenda for regular progress review meetings.

Prompt Sheet on Implementing Strategic Plans

Successful implementation of a strategy can be aided if, during the strategic planning, there is:

▪ identification of the changes needed;

▪ allocation of personal responsibilities for the implementation of the changes implied by the plan;

▪ limitation of the number of changes being pursued at any time;

▪ establishment of 'milestones' or progress measurement points;

▪ clarification of measures of performance and means of control.

Strategic changes can occur over long periods of time and can give rise to differences in the way organisations operate. As a result, the implementation of strategic changes may generate a great deal of uncertainty within the organisation. Organisations need to cope not only with the anxiety that many people experience when faced with uncertainty, but also the manic excitement that may be the less expected response of others. Strategic planning can help with the management of diverse emotional reactions by devising systems of control and regulation that ensure that tasks are clear, that their execution is monitored, that individuals and groups have the capabilities to implement the changes and that they are rewarded for doing so. The strategic plan can only be implemented through the people in the organisation. When working with people to implement plans, three aspects of the implementation will be important. These include:

Agreeing objectives – giving rewards – exercising control.

Let us now consider these in more detail.

1. Agreeing objectives

In Step 5, you formulated desirable strategic objectives for your organisation for the next few years. Some of those objectives may be given to selected staff or key managers. Other objectives may not be specific enough to be transferred so directly.

Organisations should not expect a manager or member of staff to take objectives on board without discussion. You will need to bring together the managers and staff concerned. Hopefully, they were involved in the strategic planning process and so the main points and the implications for their particular areas of responsibility should not come as a surprise. The whole organisation will need to be aware of the mission and the strategic objectives.

2. Giving rewards

Rewards include money, promotion, status and many forms of recognition and benefits in kind. Reward systems have a negative as well as a positive impact. For example, not receiving a reward can be experienced as a punishment. The timescale of a reward must match the timescale of the objective, ie, the shorter the time span of an objective, the more important it is that any incentives such as bonuses should be based on short-term measurable levels of performance.

3. Exercising control

■ You will need to consider what 'control' systems you need.

■ You will need to ask what concrete changes will appear. Can these be used to track the progress of the implementation? Choose those changes that are the clearest and most visible to most people.

■ You need to have a diverse approach to control. The choice of what changes to monitor will need to be appropriate for the people involved in that part of the plan.

▮ You need to set reasonable timescales for the change process; many changes will not occur overnight. It may take a long time to 'prime the pump' before each 'stroke pumps out progress'.

▮ Many aspects of strategy are difficult to measure quantitatively and surrogate measures must be used, eg, improved customer service might need to be monitored via a reduction in the number of complaints received, or improved morale through a reduction in graffiti or an increase in social events.

▮ You should avoid purely negative monitoring techniques, such as 'management by exceptional adverse variance'.

Prompt Sheet on Monitoring Implementation

Your organisation has little control over the environmental factors that you identified in your strategic analysis stage. As these will clearly influence the attainment of your organisation's objectives, monitoring is needed so that plans can be modified in good time.

The relationship between analysis, implementation and monitoring of results is shown below:

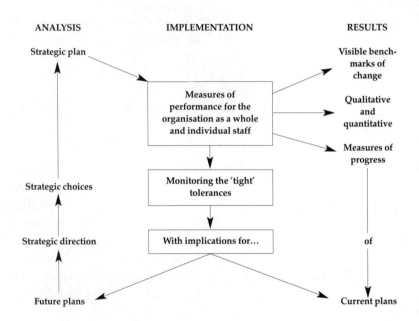

Prompt Sheet on Completing a Gantt Chart

Here is an example of a Gantt chart; it is a timetable for a couple – Simon (S) and Gillian (G) – buying a house:

Who	What	Latest start time ... How long allowed ... Finished by when ...											
		1	2	3	4	5	6	7	8	9	10	11	12
S&G	Select lender	x											
S	Qualify for mortgage		/	/									
S&G	House hunt	x	x	x	x	x							
S&G	Win bid					/	/						
S	Obtain inspections					/	/	/	/	/			
S	Obtain mortgage						/	/	/	/			
S&G	Close on house								/	/	/		
S	Find window-cleaner											x	x
S&G	Move in												/

TODAY'S DATE

How to use the chart – who should be doing what by when?

First, find today's date on the chart. Everything to the left of today's date should already be completed. In other words, all the sloping lines should be crossed through. They aren't! Who is responsible? It is Simon (S). He has not dealt with the mortgage qualification. Does it matter? Yes. It is holding up the inspection, which has not started on time. We can see that even if Simon takes immediate action, they will be three weeks late moving into the house, unless they can turn around the inspection in two weeks instead of the five weeks allowed in the plan. Perhaps Simon would have been better spending time at the building society instead of asking people about window-cleaners!

STEP 9 SUMMARY

Step 9 will have helped you to:

■ Agree an action plan

■ Decide how to reward progress

■ Decide how to monitor progress

The Next Steps

This book is divided into nine steps. If you have been able to apply each step to an organisation, then your strategic thinking has begun. You have acquired strategic skills in gathering and assessing information, in formulating strategic ideas and in planning actions to implement changes. You will now be able to think about any organisation and to give it a sense of direction. If you involve employees in helping you to answer the questions, it will be easier for them to follow your strategic thinking. The world will not stand still and your strategic thinking will continue. If you start to make changes, new information will come to light. Often it is important information that was not originally elicited. In light of this new information, you may need to modify your thinking. This book has set out a step-by-step process by which you can think about the modifications to your strategy. By working through this book, you will have developed the component thinking skills you need. With skills in strategic thinking, you will be able to make a better sense of the changing world and have a better chance of surviving those changes.

This book has been about the way that 12 specified thinking skills can be developed and combined to support strategic thinking. *Applied Thinking* (Wootton and Horne, 2004, Libra Press/Noetic Institute) details practical ways in which the 12 component thinking skills can be developed explicitly and then applied to decision making, problem solving, developing intelligence and learning from experience. Applied thinking also describes the brain research on which the work is based. The book also describes the way in which speed and accuracy of thinking can be affected by stress, mood, music, coffee, tea, food, alcohol, smoking and old age. It also describes the effects of snacks, dieting, chocolate, exercise, breathing, posture, massage, sex, sleep, smells, noises, colours, heat and ventilation, weather, photocopiers, computers and even the clothes you wear!

Readers wishing for more information can contact the authors at www.noeticinstitute.com (+44 1534 63706)